Love: Precious Moments In Time

By

Ethel Thames

ISBN: 0-7596-8528-2

This book is printed on acid free paper.

1stBooks – rev. 01/07/02

DEDICATION

I dedicate this book to the memories of
Sampson and Ethel Houston Thomas.
(Mom and Dad, I pray my book
has your approval in Heaven.)

ACKNOWLEDGEMENTS

I thank everyone: my publishing co., friends, neighbors and associates. A very special thank you to my family and to those who helped in anyway, and an extra, extra special thank you to everyone who has told me of Jesus' love.

CONTENTS

THAT SILENT NIGHT!

Star light, that shone so bright

Lead three wise men along, that night.

Where Jesus was born

In His lowly estate,

To save mankind for His goodness sake.

People gathered from near and far:

Shepherds and farmers

Followed that star…

That halt over the barn

Where the Christ child lay

Born unto us on Christmas Day!

Oh, what a feeling of peace and goodwill!

People brought gifts from far and near.

Selflessly, they gave

To the Savior, our Christ

Born unto us

That Silent Night!

THANK YOU JESUS!

THANK YOU JESUS!
THANK YOU JESUS!

THANK YOU LORD!

THANK YOU MY LORD AND
AND MY GOD!

THANK YOU THANK YOU

MY PRAYER

I'm ready, Lord

For my life to change-

I'm willing, now, to do my part.

Please fix in me

This broken spirit

And give me a brand new start.

Please, fix the way

I act each day,

Toward my fellow man

And fix in me a will to do

As much for others, as I can.

Make me your example, please…

As one who loves all

Fix me so that I'm renewed

After my demonic fall.

Make me into the sweetest gift

As anyone ever would see

And when you are finished

I'll give you, Lord,

A 'born again' me.

HOME FOR CHRISTMAS

I'm going home for Christmas!

Yes, I have my plans all made.

It's been a while

Since I've seen them all

Some memories have begun to fade.

It's time I see mom and dad, again:

Brothers and sisters, too.

We'll have a big celebration,

Just like we usually do.

Brothers are now, all grown,

And have families of their own.

One sister is engaged…

And wants me to hurry home.

I've got some news, too

It will be to their surprise;

I've been promoted on the job

Where I work to help save lives.

Dad and mom will be so happy

To have us all home once more;

We'll smell the aroma

Of mommy's Christmas baking,

Before we reach the door.

We'll each have a special ornament

To hang upon the tree;

We started this tradition,

When I was the age of three.

I'll love seeing their smiling faces

As we talk of Christmas cheer;

It's the kind of Christmas spirit,

That lasts all through the year.

I pray we'll all arrive safely

Above all we do or say;

We'll be sure that each remembers

We'll be celebrating Christ's Birthday!

We'll give thanks around the table

Then, we'll eat the food;

It will surely be to our liking;

Mommy's cooking is always so good.

We'll spend more time together

And love each other, dear;

Then, we'll hug and kiss and say good-bye

Until God brings us home next year.

I'M LONELY, BUT NOT ALONE

I'm lonely, but not alone.

Tho' I have no love

To call my own

I have whom I need, in heaven, above:

He's Father of all;

My God of Love.

When I think, sometimes,

That my faith is gone

I just wait for His lead

He is never wrong!

So, I'll be patient and I'll be strong,

And rest at His bosom

All day long.

Yes, I'll be satisfied, day by day

No earthly love

Can take His place.

My life and my loneliness,

At His feet I lay;

And just what I need-

He sends my way.

I AM WITH YOU

I am with you all the way

In what you do; in what you say.

I feel your spirit in every way;

I feel your closeness, everyday.

So Vibrant, so Great, so Wonderful

And True!

Sensitive, Intense, Omnipotent, too!

Your shinning spirit is always in view;

I try each day to be more like you.

More like you is the definite key

I will gain strength each day, you'll see;

My friends will be able

To see you in me!

As I grow in grace, in love,

And in Thee!

IT'S CLEAR

I understand, now, the joy of life

The way it was meant to be:

I put my trust in the Lord, Most High,

He makes

The difference in me!

LIFE IS A STRUGGLE

My heart inside is crying so

How much I hurt

No one knows.

The gloom and the strife

Just fills me o're

As I try hard to reach heaven's door.

I've struggled hard;

And I've tried not to whine

I accepted pain that wasn't mine.

As I try harder to walk the line-

I fall again, but, I try another time.

I'm willing to go on

And suffer this way-

I know I'll overcome the pain, one day.

I remember the Savior

Who died for my sake,

Into His hands I commend my fate.

JESUS!

He bore our sins at Calvary

T'was such a long time ago!

He cared for us, so lovingly-

Till He hung to save our souls.

How merciful of God

To give Jesus to be scourged!

And Jesus! so sweet and innocent-

Yet, He ne're said a mumbling word!

By His stripes, He healed a nation!

Now, let us live by faith!

And praise our Lord,

Our heavenly Father,

For He alone is Great!

GOD BLESS AMERICA!

God Bless America!

The country,

We, the people love:

Which shelters us from that

Which would harm,

Under the stars above.

Which travels

To the farthest shores,

And walks in the way she paves:

Which shelters us

From bombs and threats,

From lands across the waves.

Which is built

On a firm foundation:

That of God

Who sits enthroned!

Who created men as equals

God !

Who does no wrong!

God, please bless our President…

The strength of our protection;

He prays to you—Father,

Our Mighty Lord,

For his wisdom and his direction.

He sleeps with one eye open,

To be ready for the call;

To send armed forces to any shore

To defend us, one and all.

America!

Which gives her children a chance,

To be all they can be:

To rise up

From the slums of time

Into respect and dignity.

Yes, God Bless America!

Keep us in your care!

Let America be an example

To all nations—everywhere!

Long may we raise our flag!

Ever shall our dreams come true!

May it always be an honor

To live under

The red, white and blue!

Our bell shall ever ring of freedom!

If we must fight…

Then, we'll fight to save

America!

Our land of the free!

Our home of the brave!

SAFE IN HEAVEN

Each one of them left home that morning.

Whatever the reason- they had to go.

They knew that day was different

Something inside told them so.

The difference was soon made apparent:

A thunderous roar hit the work place!

Some made it home to their families

The others met God face to face.

If you try to think back—

They left a hint:

Maybe some didn't want to depart

They knew that day was different-

They felt it deep in the heart.

No enemy took your loved ones to heaven!

No airplane has ever landed there!

God brought your loved ones into heaven…

It's God who has them in His care!

Now, there are new stars in heaven.

They're out there shinning so bright-

Go out and find your special star

And tell it you'll be all right.

Then, go on; go work; go live;

Your loved ones are safe above.

There's someone here who needs you…

To bring comfort; to bring joy;

To bring love.

America!

Let's keep waving our flags;

Let's keep praying that the enemies see…

It's God who made men equal-

And it's God who makes men free.

AMERICA'S CAUSE

There, there, my little boy and my little girl!

Oh, how you cry, and how you moan!

Come, let mother comfort you,

And explain, what's going on.

Your dad, and your big brothers,

Have gone off to war:

To fight for the right,

Our country's cause.

Let us bow our heads and pray;

For dad and brothers

To come home safe, one day.

There are other families crying:

They have loved ones, too-

Who have gone to fight the war,

Just like me and you.

But, God rules over the battle;

He will see it through!

God loves all His children-

The good, the bad, too.

There are enemies around,

That seek to do some people harm.

So, dad, brothers and others are fighting,

To help insure

This harm is not done.

You see, my dear children,

America is free.

We have the right to choose as we will;

And not obey orders of those

Who just want to kill.

America is peaceful!

And would help them in their trouble…

But, they only want to see Americans buried

Under a pile of rubble.

So, we must take a stand;

And keep holding God's hand

For He is the final way!

And, what we can always, always do,

Is pray and give thanks, each day.

BYE, FOR NOW

He lay silent, now,

For he's gone away.

I'll see him soon again, some day.

He had a debt

We all must pay;

I'll see him soon,

On my 'pay' day.

HEAR MY CRY!

O, hear my cry,

With tears in my eyes!

This is more than I can bear!

For, I've lost my love;

My only love!

Now, I'm left in deep despair!

But, I know, I'll see him again, soon,

When I cross that final sea…

No other one

Can mean as much

As my love meant to me.

GOOD-BYE, DEAR FRIEND

My friend was here

All too briefly.

She suddenly went away;

But, then…

She found a new home

And a life of bliss,

Which we most pray for

At the end.

She passed away, quietly

When called through the night;

She was so meek and mild.

God needed a new angel

By dawn of day,

So, He came for

His dearly, beloved child.

She was always very kind

And had a sisterly concern for me;

We were always just as close,

As any good friends could be.

It's so hard being without

The friend I loved…

Who considered me, a blessing;

But, God knew best—

She passed His test

Now, forever is she resting.

I've often heard

Some people say,

Good friends are hard to find.

I'll leave it to God

To send me another…

Just as good and kind.

I understand,

My friend paid her cost.

Each of us

Has this to pay;

But, families and friends

Will unite again, soon…

Just let God have His way.

So, please God!

Let me live and give and love,

Let me grow and glow and pray.

Let me do your sweet bidding,

And praise

Your Holy Name!

Till you come for me, one day.

I'M WAITING

I kneel and pray to comfort

The feelings of my heart.

Mother, my dearly beloved,

From me did depart;

Up to that Isle

That blessed realm in the sky

Past the great Milky Way

Into the sweet Bye and Bye!

Rest now, Mother, dear.

Your toil of life is done;

But, for me, there's still strife

In this life beneath the sun.

I'll overcome,

I know I must go on;

And live out my days

Till my battle is won!

When God calls me home

What Glory that will be!

All the toil, the strife, the sin,

Will be gone away from me!

Once there in heaven,

I'll see you cleansed to the core:

Dressed all in white satin,

Waiting to greet me at the door.

I'll see dad and brothers,

And other cherished ones

Reaching out to welcome me—

So happy I've come.

All are rested and happy!

Not a frown on any face!

Just peace and love exuding

All over the place!

All are praising God!

All singing triumphantly!

All totally perfect, now!

All in harmony!

Glory! Glory! Glory!

Is their praise to God, Most High!

Glory! Glory! Glory!

In that sweet Bye and Bye!

OLD TROOPER

He lived almost a century.

A man of God, foremost,

He received much admiration,

And was known

From coast to coast.

He did a stint in the service,

And he fought to answer the call;

He told his fellow man

About the love of Jesus,

And how He died for us all.

He was a pioneer, like they of old,

And he helped make the world

A better place.

But, as he grew old and tired

The smile just left his face.

Then, God came and called him.

Oh, he could hear the angels sing!

He could hear

The sounding trumpets;

He could hear the gold bells ring!

He'll get the rest he truly, needs,

And he'll walk the streets of gold.

He bids this old world

Farewell, now,

To live in his heavenly, abode.

Too bad for us, if we didn't listen

When he told of Jesus' love.

Too bad for us,

If we don't confess,

And be ready when we're called above.

But, finally,

He has made it!

Oh, Glory! Glory Be!

For God reached down

And took him up!

To live for eternity!

2000's

As we say good-bye to the old years

Let's bid them a fond adieu.

We'll say, we're sorry for things unfinished,

And start this Millennium anew.

We'll stand tall among our brothers,

And keep God in every thought;

Let's tread some paths untouched before,

And live and love as we ought.

This new Millennium will challenge us,

To reach goals as never before:

First, get the homeless off our streets—

They need our help a little more.

And give the hungry a portion of meat!

Think! What if they were we?

Lord, help us—that we may help them!

It's the way our world should be!

Remember to cheerily greet our fellow man,

And bid his day be good;

Say hello or shake hands as we stroll about,
With those in the neighborhood.

Let's build and produce, as we were meant to;
And enjoy this Millennium as we live.
Salute those who fought; it was they who bought,
Our freedom with all they could give.

Whether life is long or short,
Live it to the fullest each day!
Be silent for awhile and give our thanks—
Remember to always pray.

Come on, let's get started!
Away with hostility and sneers!
But, with brotherhood and praise;
And reaching out each day
We start these Millennium years.

THE OLD FOLKS HOME AT GARDEN SQUARE

There's a beautiful home, called Garden Square.

Someone told me, that old folks live there.

It's a spacious place, of scenery and sun;

Where some old folks live, till their days are done.

It's over the hill, in a chosen spot

A good man gave; he wasn't using the lot.

Just the right place

For some old folks to rest;

While waiting on earth, for their final quest.

I passed there again, the other day;

I stopped and spent time,

Before going on my way.

I met some old folks, and lent them a hand;

The feeling I derived was truly, grand!

Some old folks were playing; trying to have fun:

Some, sat under trees, avoiding the sun

One picked roses, and gave me one;

Her eyes were tired; her face was worn.

"Here," she said, "a rose for you."

I reached for the rose, and took her hand, too.

She smiled and said, "What a tender touch!"

I thanked her, and said, 'I love the rose, so much!'

Another I met was a bit confused;

But, we laughed, and talked,

As we pitched horseshoes.

He became tired; I helped him to his quarter;

He told each one we met

That I was his daughter.

Then, I heard singing going on,

In the chapel;

The sound was not the greatest of tone;

But, God, these old folks know!

Yes, they know—

You'll never leave them alone!

As I visited around, before going on my way,

I thanked God

That I took time that day;

To show mercy and kindness,

To some lonely old souls…

Still God's children;

Even when they're old!

One day, who knows, maybe I'll live there.

I'd want someone to visit—

I'd need someone to care;

I may live out my life, with some of them there…

At the old folks home, called Garden Square.

A TASK OF HEART

I reached out for the comfort

Of your touch;

But, alas, you were not there.

Thoughts of your sweetness

Run wildly through my mind;

Dear, you know how much I care.

I'm falling apart for want of you;

Yet, we can't be together, now…

You have a task of heart to complete,

Before our hearts can be bound.

But, if wishing and hoping

Could bring you near;

Then, you are ever close.

How I'll survive

Till we'll together again, dear;

Really, only heaven knows.

A SPECIAL SOMEONE

Everyone needs a special someone

In his life…

The one whom he thinks

Makes his life complete.

Pray for your

Someone.

A SWEET SONG OF LOVE

A sweet song of love, is what I hear,

The moment you come near.

Be still my heart is what I say,

To keep from shedding a tear.

Just look at you, is what I do

For, in my life, you're prime.

I run to you; embrace my love;

As I do all the time.

It's deeper, now that we are one;

With a dearer and sweeter love.

We have a little one on the way

Sent from heaven, above.

For years to come, as we shall grow,

In love, in happiness, and in grace;

We'll live our lives in one accord

As we have promised in faith.

AN ACCOUNT FROM A NEXT OF KIN

Here's an account from a next of kin;

Who just about slipped off the very deep end…

"Sometimes, I just want to holler and scream.

It's because of a nightmare, or some odd thing…

People I know, think I'm so mean;

But, I live my life

Down life's mean stream.

Maybe, it's the rage, I feel in my head.

The times are tough; my bills are in the red.

I gotta get up, and get my family fed;

My wife keeps nagging me

And pulling on the spread.

Well, I tried and tried, to get myself a job;

But, no one hired me

Till I met this guy, Bob.

When he said "yes", I started to sob;

He said, "Clean up your act,

And don't be a slob."

"I cleaned up my act;

I got rid of my rage;

Stopped dreaming bad dreams;

I acted the man of my age…

They hired me at the warehouse,

As a general aide;

And at the end of the week, haha!

I got paid.

I took home some groceries;

Bought my wife a new dress;

Bought the children new shoes;

That relieved so much stress…

I paid on some bills,

And gave the landlord the rest;

I've promised myself,

To keep doing my best.

The warehouse is big

And the hard work hurts;

I get tired of the lifting, the pulling

And the dirt;

But, I've got a strong back,

And I'll tough it out…

Keeping my family fed,

Is now what I'm about.

My story goes on, but, you get my drift;

I was given a break;

That made all the diff'rence.

We shout hallelujahs, this fine day…

And we're learning to lean

And we're learning to pray.

We do what we can,

To pass kindness along;

We teach our children

To be faithful and strong…

You can't live in this world

And make it on your own…

A loving, helping hand,

Gave my heart a new song.

CHERISH ME ALWAYS

Hide me

In the shelter of your loving arms

Sing to me

While I drink of your dearest charms

Talk to me

As I nestle close to your heart

And

Love me forever

Lest I fall apart.

Graciously accept

That my love for you is deep

Tell me you love me

Each night before we sleep

Wake me with the kiss

That makes my joy complete…

And

To cherish me always

Is your promise to keep.

COME GET MY LOVE

The love I have for you is waiting

In my heart.

Love that you are missing,

Since misunderstanding

Keeps us apart.

I stay awake at night

Like a lovelorn, so blue;

I'm the one you need, dear

My heart beats just for you.

When I was up and you were down…

I lovingly nourished your heart.

I'm here now hoping and praying

To keep us from falling apart.

But, I'll be patient and I'll be kind

And keep my love warm for you.

You'll see in time, I'm whom you need…

I'm here, I'm waiting,

And I'm true.

COME HOME, MY LOVE

Come home my love

From across the seas,

To this love you left behind.

Come to me

While I dream so sweet;

Wake me with love divine.

I burn at night

With that certain yearning…

I toss and turn

Till I'm tired and worn.

I pray each day

You'll come home safe,

Soon, some blessed morn.

Here in the mist of dreamland;

I place a kiss on my love's face.

Please, God!

Just let me wake and find myself…

Wrapped in his tender embrace.

DADDY'S NEW BABY BOY

Daddy sits little baby

On his knee.

Dad wants to play a game

With little 'D'.

But baby seems to enter

This stirring plea:

"Please, daddy, please,

Let me get some sleep!

I've been on a hard journey

The last day or two…

And your boy is so sleepy

He doesn't know what to do.

After a little while

It can be just me and you.

Then, we can play peek-a-boo,

Or whatever you want to.

Right now,

Your little baby needs his rest…

Give me time to be at my best.

I'll be more alert

In an hour or two

Then, D will be happy

To play with you."

"Well, sleep, my little baby,"

Is what daddy said,

"I must have been a little bit

Out of my head.

The journey you've traveled

Was hard, it's true…

But, you've ended one journey

And have started one new.

I love you my son,

Honest I do.

I'll be loyal and strong,

A good daddy for you.

We'll play, and we'll pray,

And we'll go to the zoo,

And I'll always thank God

For giving me—you.

We'll travel life's highways

Searching for various views…

So you see, little D,

Your path is fixed, somewhat for you.

There is so much in life

For you to do.

And as you grow up,

You'll find this to be true.

So, yes, rest sweet baby…

Everything will be fine.

And daddy's here for you,

When you have time."

FILLED UP ON YOU

As I walk in the rain, I think of you,

And it fills my heart with delight-

I'll have the love I've waited for,

Return to me tonight.

What am I, without the love,

That makes me void of tears?

You are the light that woke my soul,

From darkness and from fears.

My thoughts of you

Bring laughter in the rain,

For it's truly, such a pleasure…

To have the love my soul desires,

And that my dear heart treasures.

So, welcome home, dearly beloved,

To arms opened wide;

And to a heart

That's waiting and wanting,

To be rescued

From dying in side.

GOOD-NIGHT, DEAR

Soft as the sap that drips from the tree;

As tasty as the honey, made by the bee…

Sweet as the cane, that the farmers reap…

Is the kiss you place on my lips,

Each night I lay me down

To sleep.

GOOD EXERCISE

Every morning and every night,

I get up and exercise.

I don't want the bulge in my thighs-

And I don't want to be criticized.

I move up, then, I move back

My head erect, my shoulders relaxed,

On three and four

I change my track…

And on one and two, I'm a jumping jack.

As I move around, I do something else

Hey, guys…

I'm getting beside myself!

With one side-straddle, and then, a hop

I'm happy for the spunk I've got!

Before too long, I'll achieve my goal,

If I maintain this solid hold

Enjoying life like never before…

With a one, and a two

And a three and a four,

With a one, and a two

And a three and a four.

GUESS WHO

He has soft, beautiful hair,

And strong arms and legs.

A well-rounded body,

A beautifully shapped head.

His fingers and toes

Are a little chubby,

And he has a smile

That drives me wild!

Just who is this beautiful being?

Why—

He's my little sweet

Grandchild!

I MUST BE PATIENT

If I had someone to hold,

I wouldn't faint so much

If I had his arms around me;

If I could feel his tender touch…

Then my days wouldn't be so hard,

And my hours wouldn't seem so long.

I'd be glad at the work day's end,

So, that I could hurry home.

For, the light of my life would be there!

Waiting with opened arms!

To enwrap my spirit with his own,

And bathe me with his charms.

Oh, how long have I waited?

Will this be my day?

Will I meet the one, I've dreamed about?

Will he come my way?

I must be patient, and I must wait,

Until my time comes around.

I know my love, wherever he is;

Will wait till his true love is found.

IT'S LOVE

You have comforted my heart with love,

Like none before,

The magic of the simple things

Is the joy that fills me o're.

My love for you keeps growing

And each breath of life I breathe…

Is more important to me now

So, my heart can rest with ease.

May we always be guided

By wisdom from above,

And be for each other the star

That lights our hearts with love.

I THOUGHT OF YOU

I thought of you again, my dear,

As I do everyday.

I transfer myself into your mist

To look upon your face:

For the light, the warmth,

The love you exude-

Your gentle style and grace…

For dear, I feel the warmest ever,

When I'm in your strong embrace.

I'M GRATEFUL TO YOU, OLD FRIEND

I looked my old friend squarely

In the face.

I could clearly see, how much she has aged.

Beyond the wrinkles, and her smile, so wide,

I can see something, she can not hide.

There is something I must to tell her,

That I have put off…

Because, I know she understands me,

Even when we don't talk.

But my love and my gratitude,

I must express

Before God takes her home,

To her long awaited rest.

I may be called, before the setting sun,

So I won't continue,

To let this go undone.

She calls me 'honey', 'sweet' and 'dear',

And is so kind to me...

More, with each passing year.

I must speak now and make it clear-

My love and my gratitude

While, still she can hear.

So many times, we wait too late,

To give our flowers

Before death's date.

I will tell her now- today is the day!

This is the message I shall convey:

'You've been here for me, all the way.

I cried on your shoulders,

After my many mistakes...

With your wonderful wisdom

You helped set me straight.

Dear friend, I love you;

And I thank you.'

Now! to those of you,

Who've been like this...

Never a kind word, a big hug or a kiss.

Express your love and gratitude

While you can…

Life is too short to keep holding it in!

So, while the sweet breath of life

Still flows in your friend,

And even if you need

To make up with your kin,

Give love, gratitude and flowers

With a big grin

And never wait as long

To express your feelings, again.

IT HURTS

You've taken your love to someone new

And left me alone in pain.

I feel so deeply

Just thinking of you,

Till it hurts to say your name.

It's said that all good things must end,

And, sometimes, even love dies.

Time is too precious to fuss and fight,

So, never build a life on lies.

More power to you-

More power to me,

As onward and upward we go.

Maybe, in time, I'll love once more,

When my heart heals-

And again, opens its door.

IT'S CRAZY, BUT

It's crazy, but, when my love is near

I get so excited, until I can't see clear.

I can't stand up and I can't sit down-

I don't know what to do

So, I act like a clown.

I wiggle, I giggle, I fumble and coo;

I wobble and goggle;

Do you do this, too?

I often do this…when I should do that

It's crazy, yes, but that's how I act.

I beg my heart to let me be

Excited and delighted, but with dignity;

To receive love sweetly

Into my heart

And return love gently,

Without falling apart.

I PLEDGE MY LOVE

As your chosen one; I pledge to you,

Love to the end.

I will walk by your side; hold your hand

And be your best friend.

I'll try hard to always smile,

And keep our love from growing thin

And be the one whom you can trust

And have confidence in.

As you pledge the same thing, too…

We'll work together

To keep our love brand new.

We'll live our lives from day to day

In the Light of God's love,

And in the wisdom of His way.

I NEED YOU

I need you to be so close to me,

Fulfilling each dream, I've ever dreamed

Massaging my soul in harmony,

To the beautiful melody

My heart sings.

Hold me in your loving arms…

Whisper sweetly to me

Or sing my song.

While the moment is still

And the night is calm

Let's give in to the feelings

That have been so strong.

Then, we'll float gently

Down the stream of time…

Creating new memories,

For the ties that bind.

Side by side,

With every mountain we climb

Always together; keeping love kind.

LOVE COUNTS

You're always teasing me about this or that

You have quite a comic view.

Your mind is always on lighter things

I really love this about you.

But, when things come up

On the stronger side of life

You know when to put play aside

And help me deal with things

Above my head-

My darling, you're my strength

And my guide.

One lost soul, this girl would be

Were it not for your love alone.

You reached out and rescued me,

And brought me safely home.

And truly, I hope I am for you

Just what you need me to be.

I want you strong, and happy,

And always growing…

And always

Here beside me.

LOVE IS WHAT WE NEED

Love is what we need more of

So darling, I'll begin with you…

Never want of love and affection

As long as I'm in view.

LOVE RENEWED

I listened as you talked to me

You told me things I wanted to hear:

How lovely are my eyes,

How beautiful is my smile,

And how you love me so dear.

We know our love was meant to be,

Our hearts have made that clear.

We've endured the pain

Of the strain of love

And we've overcomed the fear.

Now that our hearts beat

Together again,

We'll forget the wasted years…

Our lives are happy and strong enough,

To wipe away all the tears.

LOVE'S PROMISE

Let the light in your eyes illumine me

My soul hungers for your love.

Let your lips cover my every longing,

As I gaze into the stars, above.

And let your loving arms surround me,

Holding me close, while we dance;

As the maestro waves his baton,

To start the music of the band.

When your body clings close to mine,

I feel that we are one

A-mid a crowd of thousands present,

Yet, to us, there is none.

Enfold me and forever love me,

As we live as it was meant to be:

Our minds submerged in love divine,

And beautiful harmony.

LOVE IS FOREVER

You say you want to leave our union,

Because love has grown a bit stale.

It really hurts to hear these words,

So much, I can not tell.

Love is more than just the passion, dear,

It's the commitment we made at the start.

Now, you turn,

And walk away, so easily

And leave me with a broken heart.

Maybe it's good

That you leave for awhile!

But, think on what we've shared:

The sickness, the health,

The wealth of life;

And the love we both declared.

I pray, in time

Your heart will change,

And you'll want to mend this tare…

We'll keep our commitment

Of love and honor

With never another snare.

MY VALENTINE

By the way, dear,

In case you just didn't know.

You are my sweetest Valentine

I'm happy I've told you so!

MAMA, AND LITTLE BABY

Little baby wakes from her nap,

Not seeing her mother, she cries.

Mama rushes in to comfort her,

And wipes her weeping eyes.

"Gu-gu, ga-ga, mama!"

Is little baby's resounding verse.

"Okay! my darling daughter…"

Then, mama lets her baby nurse.

As baby nestles on mama's arm,

Mama knows she wouldn't trade this

For the world!

Being a loving and devoted mom,

And receiver of baby's love.

Majestic sweetness is the picture

Of mama

And her precious pearl!

And surely, God made this to be…

Mama, and her little baby girl.

MOTHER

She would combed my hair

With loving care;

She would make sure

My braids were straight.

Then, she'd put on me

The loveliest dress

And, oh, I felt so great!

She'd cook the meals

And clean the house,

And I'd help put things in place…

Then, we'd walk and talk

As she guided my life

And she'd give me

The sweetest embrace.

But, of all the memories

Of the loveliest life,

That anyone has ever saved;

I shall never forget

The warmest feeling of all…

When me and mommy

Knelt and prayed.

MY GRANDSON

He's a happy, energetic little boy:

So bold, so beautiful, so grand!

My heart is lifted when I see him playing,

Or when he reaches out and takes my hand…

Ooh, I just lift him off the floor,

And dance around with him in my arms!

And oow the smile and the loving charm,

He has for me, his dearest grandmom.

We continue our time,

With more fun and games;

And I bounce him up and down on my lap…

Then, I say a little pray with him,

And lay him down for his nap.

Pretty soon, we're at it again!

There's nothing I love more!

A very special little gift from God…

To help rear, secure and adore.

And I wonder…

Will I live to see him grow?

Will I see him take a stand?

Maybe I'll be called to heaven's door,

Before he becomes a man.

But, for now,

I'll be with him and love him…

And help when he's in a jam.

I pray to be here or close around,

When he needs his dear, old gram.

But, should I get my final call…

Just when I am so blest!

Please, God!

Keep him at your bosom…

When I am called to rest.

MY EYES GET MISTY

My eyes get misty, when I think of you-

Of the time we met; and of how we grew,

And of all the things we two, would do…

Make my eyes misty, to think of you.

You have grown so in mind, it's true,

And accomplished so much-

You are too cool!

I sit here wondering, and thinking of you;

My best friend,

When we were kids in school.

If you're wondering about me…

Well, from my point of view,

I've done things

To make my life improve

I've turned some things around

And I've made some things new;

Still my eyes get misty

When I think of you.

I'm sure many times,

You think of me and grin;

Remembering the time,

We stepped off the deep end…

They thought we were a bit crazy,

But, we were just good friends;

Trying to make 'um laugh',

But, they didn't comprehend.

We were quite athletic

And head strong, too;

Remember the races we won,

When they said we were through?

Well, we knew we could win

And we determined to!

We were something else, then-

That, indeed, is true.

Remember also, our Spanish class…

We tried to speak Spanish,

And all that jazz;

Even the teacher

broke down and laughed—

Yea, we were 'los burros'

Of the Spanish class.

Many thought we would lose out

On life's race.

Some thought we were a lost case;

But, we've gone on

And we've made the grade.

The memories of you, friend,

Will not fade.

Those times were wonderful

And all too few.

We, both, really had some growing to do;

I did all right, and so did you…

Hats off to those

Who helped us make it through.

NEW ARRIVAL

Everyone's excited

That he's almost here—

Wee baby is struggling

Hard to come!

If mommy bears down,

Just one more time…

Wee baby will be born by dawn.

NEWBORN

Baby, Doryin Isaiah,

With those bright, brown eyes…

Oh, how we love

Your angelic smile!

You delight our hearts,

Each and everyone—

You brought joy to our lives

Where there was none.

We acknowledge God,

Who sent you to us-

We love our Lord,

And in Him, we trust.

You were in a plan, not made by man,

As you pass our hands…

Grow as strong as you can.

We love you, dear baby,

And we respect you.

You must love, obey and respect us, too.

So that your days may be filled
With the joys of your heart…
Love, honor
And delight yourself in God.

But, right now, darling…
Sleep and play while you can,
Because life brings tests-
It's in the plan.

You must pass these tests
And help make things right;
As you govern or preach…
Whichever you might.

May God ever bless you,
Your dear ones, too,
And fill us with wisdom
On how to rear you.

As you grow strong,

And take longer strides in life—

May you be what this world needs

To help bring us

Closer to Christ.

THE PROPOSAL

When at last, he said he loved me…

Oh, it gave my heart a start!

No more did I have to nudge him,

To make him say, what seemed so hard.

After that…

There was no stopping him,

And he said we'd never part.

Then, he asked me to marry him,

And pledged to me, his heart.

The proposal I have waited for…

He uttered on bended knee!

"Darling, will you marry me?"

Is just the way he asked me.

The light of day, just opened wide!

Oh, how the sun did shine!

At last, he asked me to marry him…

We toasted our engagement with wine.

I'd always said my prayers…

That this would happened soon!

And truly, God has answered me!

We marry tomorrow, at noon.

SECURED LOVE

Yes, it's true, I'm in love with him!

He has absolutely stolen my heart!

He's a man of strength and duty;

Not easily torn apart.

Yet, such gentleness he exudes!

And he's my gentle king.

I see my dreams all coming true,

Because I'm wearing his ring!

Yes!

He asked me to be his own…

He wants me to be part of his life!

He said we'd ride the clouds together,

If I would be his sweet wife!

My eyes light up when I see him!

I break into the 'slo mo' race!

Into his arms, he captures me,

And holds me in his manly embrace.

For real! I answered yes to him!

What a difference he's made in my life!

Yes, I will marry you, darling, dear!

It would honor me,

To be your sweet wife!

SOFTLY KISS ME

Softly kiss me, dear-

Just the way I like

Softly kiss me, and hold me tight.

Soothe my woes and pains,

All through the night,

And softly kiss me

Till the morning light.

There's an ache in my heart

That time has not healed

I can not rejoice,

Until this ache disappears.

Love on me tenderly

All through the night,

And softly kiss me,

Till the morning light.

You have the touch that I need

That is more solid than gold.

It warms my heart,

And shields it from cold.

Please, love on me and hold me,

Make my life new and bold!

Let your love fill me

And relieve my heavy load!

Our hearts shall meet,

And beat out love's old ache.

Love on me tenderly,

Don't let my heart break!

Hold me ever so close,

And hold me ever so tight…

And softly kiss me,

Till night comes to light.

Your gentleness,

And sweet tenderness

Make life easier to bear;

The warm breath that you breathe,

As you hover over me,

Leaves me with never a care!

Darling, attend my mind!

Don't worry about time!

For still we have all night.

Come upon me please,

With all gentleness and ease;

Enwrap me with pure delight!

Comes light of day,

Let's break away,

And do the bidding

That each day brings;

Bear in mind,

This heart that pines,

Still yearns to gaily sing.

Then, let's begin anew

When the day's work is through,

And you come

Unto me sweetly

And do what I like

Love and hold me tight…

And softly kiss me

Till morning, again,

Comes to light.

SWEET LOVE

I'm thankful for the time we've had,

To make our love brand new;

But, darling, dear,

Did you ever think-

I could stop loving you?

TIME WILL TELL

You are what I need, my love,

Forever and a day.

You fill my days and nights, more full

Of meaning, in every way.

And maybe, dear, as time shall pass

You'll feel the same way, too…

And say the same, sweet words to me,

As I have said to you.

TOGETHER, AGAIN

Tomorrow, darling, I'll see your sweet face

So, I can't get to sleep, tonight.

Just thinking of our love embrace,

Overwhelms me with sheer delight.

The enchanted closeness,

We'll relive, very soon;

Is why I lie awake

I'm reliving the love life we have had

That made my body quiver and quake.

A very gentle feeling,

Is what's in store for you

I know so well, my darling, dear…

That you feel the same way, too.

Our love is coming together

And that soothes my state of mind…

Our hearts will melt

With the gentlest love

Of the most endurable kind.

TRUE LOVE

When I awake each morning

With your warm body next to mine,

Joy overcomes my being

To claim love so kind.

In such hard times,

And struggles galore,

You took on my problems, too…

How blessed am I

To surely claim love,

So rare and oh, so true!

TO SEE YOU NOW!

Oh, to see you now; I long for you so!

I try to stay busy—keep things in order,

But, time is still too slow.

It's the thought of you that fills me

With that radiant glow, you love,

And I pray each day to heaven

To thank our Lord, above.

In your work, it's true

You fill a great capacity;

I dream I'm in your arms each night,

Clinging!

With great tenacity!

But, there's a song of love-

Written especially for us, two;

It keeps our memories alive and well,

And keeps our love strong and new.

It keeps me walking

With my head held high

And helps me that I will not roam.

My darling, I know,

When you're done across the seas…

Then, soon again, you'll be home.

WHY OH WHY?

Why, oh why, did I say no,

When the boy asked

If he could be my beau?

Was it my heart?

Or was it my mouth?

Or was it because

We were in a crowd?

For me to say, no…

Just goes to show,

That when we mean yes,

We often say, no.

But, if he gives me a chance,

I'll tell him so;

That I meant yes…

When I said, no.

WHAT WOULD I DO?

"What would I ever do

If love didn't live anymore"?

That's what he asked his girl,

As he was leaving her door…

"But, love is alive

And will live for evermore"!

Is the answer she gave…

And then, closed the door.

WHAT A PLEASURE!

How radiant are your eyes

And the smile on your face!

The way you walk,

The way you talk,

Your certain style and grace;

All show that you are a boy in love,

And oh, how easy to see!

The pleasure is mine;

I toast you with wine!

For your affections

Are showered upon me!

YOU MAKE MY HEART SING

Dear, if ever a heart

Did rejoice and sing,

It was my heart

When you gave me your ring:

The symbol of love that has no end…

You and I together

Is the message it sends.

That you chose me to marry

And to wear your ring;

Lifts my heart and makes it sing.

I rejoice for the happiness

And thank God, above…

The Giver of life;

The Epitome of love.

YOU ARE THE REASON

If you need me to tell you;

Then, you are all I desire.

You are what makes me,

My very best self…

Yes, my darling,

You are the reason why.

MASTER OF DECEPTION

You! Master of Deception, Devil, by name!

How long on this earth,

Will you play your games?

You wear so many faces;

Yet, none of them is true.

In no way, do your many faces,

Describe the real you.

You catch many people unaware;

It's really quite a shame…

Too many fall, for nothing at all;

They can't beat you at your game.

You crawl, you creep, you even sneak…

You're a real scuz bucket, it's true!

But, Master of Deception,

I'm here to say,

That I am on to you!

I spent too much time, as I went along,

Following after you for my pleasure;

But, I saw the light!

Thank God for that night!

Righteousness is now what I treasure!

So, get thee behind me!

I'm done with you!

You've had me from my youth!

God changed my ways…

My feet are staid!

Now, I belong to Truth!

ABOUT THE AUTHOR

Ethel Thames, a first time author, was born, raised and educated in Jackson, Mississippi. She received her B.S. Degree from Jackson State College and taught school a few years in Mississippi before making her home in Sandusky, Ohio, where she is wife, mother and grandmother. She enjoys such hobbies as sketching, collecting sports cards and old cameras and writing poetry.

www.ingramcontent.com/pod-product-compliance
Ingram Content Group UK Ltd.
Pitfield, Milton Keynes, MK11 3LW, UK
UKHW041937190726
13854UKWH00004B/1630